DIY

ART AND CRAFT FOR SENIOR CITIZENS

SIMPLE, FUN AND HEALTHY CREATIVE ACTIVITIES

Kim Banks

NINE

Get Artful

One

Introduction

Searching for an innovative and pleasant method for investing your free energy? Look at our broad rundown of artworks for seniors. It incorporates an extensive variety of art exercises, from painting and weaving to carpentry and scrapbooking. Anything your inclinations or expertise level, there are many ways of having some good times while keeping your hands involved and your inventiveness prospering.

Did you have any idea that creating offers various advantages for more seasoned individuals? Being taken part in active imaginative exercises can work on coordinated movements, fortify social associations, diminish pressure, and lighten uneasiness. It can likewise be great for the mind. An exploration concentrated on in the Diary of Neuropsychiatry and Clinical Neurosciences found that seniors who partook in creates like stoneware and weaving had a lower chance of creating gentle mental impedance.

Furthermore, in a Mental Science study, seniors who figured out how to stitch or do computerized photography showed further developed memory capability. So, making specialties might be an extraordinary method for keeping your cerebrum invigorated and improving your mental capacities.

Additionally, numerous seniors who have actual limits can in any case encounter the delights of making by adjusting the exercises or utilizing extraordinary gear. For instance, more established grown-ups who like to weave can utilize bigger needles and heavier yarn. The people who appreciate carpentry however experience issues standing or utilizing power instruments can find a seat at a table and collect undertakings from units. Furthermore, established crafters with vision difficulties can utilize amplifying to help.

We've gathered together more than 50 of the best specialty thoughts for seniors and assembled them into direct classifications to assist you with rapidly finding what you're keen on:

Two

General Art work Thoughts

Is it true that you are prepared to get creative? Whether you're searching for projects that utilization paper, glass, wood, blossoms, or dabs, you're certain to be motivated by this rundown. Look at these straightforward art thoughts for more seasoned grown-ups:

- Suncatchers: Make your home shimmer by creating a suncatcher to hang in your window. You can make a lightweight suncatcher out of bricklayer container covers and shading sheets or go somewhat heavier and use glass stones. You could actually make one utilizing softened dabs.
- Scrap-texture magnets: Need a charming method for spending those old pieces of texture? Add a touch of felt and transform them into charming ladybug magnets.
- Dirt gems charms: Make individual of-a-sort adornments pieces by forming your own special charms out of polymer mud. Adding a switch catch to your neckband will

make it more straightforward to put on and take off.

- Squeezed blossoms: Accumulate a few blossoms and orchestrate them inventively between two sheets of wax paper. Put a weighty book on top to overload the blossoms and allow it to sit for the time being. When the blossoms are absolutely level, you can cover them or use them to enhance welcoming cards, bookmarks, napkins, photograph edges, and that's just the beginning.

- Aviaries: Building things out of wood can profoundly fulfill. In the event that you have the proper devices and expertise, you can fabricate a perching space without any preparation.

  Another choice is to collect one from a locally acquired pack.

- Beaded wristbands: Utilizing security pins and brilliantly shaded globules, you can make some modified bling and wear it with satisfaction.

- Wind rings: Wind tolls can be a vivid and enchanting expansion to a nursery. What about a straightforward plan that utilizes earth pots with previous openings?
- Paper blossoms: Light up any room with blossoms that you make yourself. You can make wonderful sprouts out of tissue paper or espresso channels.
- Welcoming cards: Custom made cards are an incredible method for telling friends and family you're pondering them. You can utilize paper, stickers, texture, strips, and numerous different materials to make fun and inventive cards for any event, like Christmas, birthday events, or Easter.

Three

Sewing, Weaving, And Stitching Specialties

Needlecrafts like weaving and sewing are the absolute most well-known exercises among more seasoned grown-ups. That is somewhat in light of the fact that they require negligible hardware and should frequently be possible from the solace of an easy chair. You can partake in these sorts of exercises in your brilliant years. Truth be told, English cause Sew for Harmony studied in excess of 1,000 knitters and observed that more than 66% of them were beyond 60 years old, and many were in their 80s and 90s.

The following are a couple of thoughts for the sake of entertainment needlecraft projects:

✓ Book cover: Safeguard your number one books and add a little wonder to your racks by sewing a vivid book cover. A sewing machine makes the work go speedier, yet you can likewise line your book cover manually.

- ✓ Warming pack: Utilizing texture and some rice, you can make microwavable warming sacks to assist with calming your throbbing painfulness. You might add medicinal balms for some fragrance-based treatment.
- ✓ Toss cushions: Add a sprinkle of variety to your couch with some simple to-make toss pads. For a greater extent a test, take a stab at adding a few beautifying trims like tufts or ribbon.
- ✓ Pillowcase: Change the vibe of a room by sewing a pillowcase to embellish any style.
- ✓ Dish material: Sewed dish fabrics are really helpful and make incredible gifts. Furthermore, they're basic enough that they can frequently be done in a solitary sitting.
- ✓ Espresso comfortable: Stay away from scorchs by sewing or knitting a delicate fleece cover to put around a warm cup.

- ✓ Memory quilt: Here's an incredible approach to reuse old materials: Make a customized memory quilt from old shirts, child covers, a wedding dress, or even a tactical uniform

Four

Painting And Shading Artworks

Numerous seniors appreciate communicating their thoughts with markers and paint brushes. Zeroing in on examples and varieties quiets the psyche and permits the cerebrum to enjoy some time off from day to day stresses. Truth be told, some examination proposes that shading can affect the body as contemplation. In view of that, look at these instances of painting and shading projects for seniors:

- ➢ Shading Books for Grown-ups: Shading isn't only for youngsters! Grown-up shading books are an undeniably well-known way for seniors to unwind, assuage pressure, and make something delightful. Huge print shading books for grown-ups with low vision are additionally accessible.

- ➢ Mathematical tape painting: Utilize painter's tape on a piece of material to check mathematical lines in an example, paint between the tape lines, then, at that point, eliminate the tape. This can be an incredible way for seniors with insecure hands to deliver a composition with pleasant smooth edges.

➢ Painted rocks: Your creative mind is as far as possible with regards to painting rocks. You can transform rocks into ladybugs, garden markers, and significantly more.

➢ Painted mirrors: On the off chance that you have an old mirror with an edge that has been better, take a stab at giving it a new existence with some shower paint.

➢ Earthenware pots: Add a little energy to common nursery pots. You can paint them freehand or utilize a stencil to add subtleties like hearts, leaves, or stars.

➢ Pine cones: Painted pine cones can make a beautiful expansion to any focal point.

➢ Watercolor illuminating presences: Need a vivid method for illuminating your yard or deck? With a touch of paint, some espresso channels, and a bricklayer container, you can make a lovely illuminator.

Five

Photograph Crafts

Integrating photographs into creates is a definitive method for customizing a task. Numerous seniors appreciate taking pictures, and some have boxes of photographs gathering dust in a storage room, some place that could be effectively utilized. On the off chance that you have computerized photographs on a memory card, cell phone, or PC, you can print them out yourself or have them printed decently cheaply at a nearby mall.

Photographs make very great gifts since they are so private. Think about these thoughts:

- ❖ Scrapbook: Making a scrapbook is a superb method for safeguarding recollections. Let your inventiveness free and utilize papers, strips, stickers, and different embellishments to beautify your pages.
- ❖ Montage board: Make a one of a kind wall decoration by orchestrating a lot of your most loved photographs in a covering design

and sticking them to wood, material, or corkboard.

❖ Photograph magnets: Transform your ice chest into a photograph exhibition! With cement attractive sheets, it's not difficult to make magnets out of photographs of any size.

❖ Photograph shape: Photograph 3D squares are a pleasant method for showing a lot of photographs in a little region, and they make extraordinary discussion pieces. It's ideal to pick photographs that will function admirably as squares.

❖ Photograph liners: Need a viable method for flaunting a portion of your number one prints? Stick them on liners and put them out for your next get-together.

❖ Photograph covered vase: Carry an individual touch to a standard window box. You can let the photographs represent themselves or add different subtleties like a significant expression or saying.

Six

Christmas Art Work For Seniors

Creating is one of the most outstanding ways of showing your vacation soul by adding a merry touch to your environmental elements. Take a shot at one of these Christmas makes for seniors:

- Pumpkin seed poinsettia: Use pumpkin seeds, paste, and splash paint to make an exemplary Christmas blossom that can be held tight a tree or worn as a pin.
- Sock snowman: A lovable snowman is easy to assemble with provisions you likely have lying around the house. You can make it significantly more straightforward by utilizing versatile groups as opposed to string.
- Make stick snowflakes: You've likely heard that no two snowflakes are indistinguishable. Utilize your creative mind to make an interesting snowflake

configuration out of wooden specialty sticks.

- Cupcake liner tree decoration: With a touch of collapsing and sticking, merry cupcake liners can undoubtedly turn into a hanging Christmas tree. Painted espresso channels would likewise work for this art.
- Tea light snowman: Battery-worked tea lights can become beguiling snowmen decorations in a couple of basic advances.
- Bow wreath: Add some seasonal happiness to your front entryway with an innovative wreath made of gift bows.

Seven

Other Occasion Specialties

From Halloween and Thanksgiving to Valentine's Day and Easter, Father's Day and Mother's Day exceptional events merit unique specialty thoughts. Examine these models:

- ✓ Fall leaf light holders: Gather up a portion of those wonderful fall leaves, get a couple glass shakes, and make glass flame holders for your Thanksgiving focal point.
- ✓ Paper plate holder jack-o'- lamp: Shower paint and felt is everything necessary to transform a woven paper plate holder into an exemplary Halloween character. You can utilize it on your table or balance it on a wall.
- ✓ Pom pumpkins: Commend the fall by making these out of control pumpkins out of yarn and a couple of embellishments.
- ✓ Heartfelt decoration: In the event that you're great with a needle and string, take a stab at reusing some old fleece sweaters into these basic weaved heart

trimmings. Felt fortune treats: Treat your friends and family to a custom-made fortune treat this Valentine's Day. No baking!

- ✓ Little treat button Art: Here's an imaginative (and charming) method for utilizing that large number of old buttons: Paste them into the state of a ball and casing the outcome

Eight

Simple Specialties to Do with Grandkids

Making creates is a magnificent method for uniting the ages. Here are a few straightforward undertakings that you can make with youthful ones:

- ➢ Stick arm bands: Wooden specialty sticks can make incredible wristbands, yet this art requires a touch of prep work: You really want to heat up the sticks, shape them, and let them dry for the time being before you can embellish them.
- ➢ Tissue paper stained glass: With a straightforward pack, you and the youthful ones can make delightful stained-glass plans utilizing just tissue paper and paste. Another choice is to make the layouts yourself out of dark cardstock.
- ➢ Clothespin vehicle: Vivid vehicles made of clothespins and buttons are not difficult to assemble and are a wonderful method for keeping little hands occupied.

- ➤ Terrarium: Make a beautifying garden in a glass compartment. For additional tomfoolery, let the children add plastic dinosaurs, elves, or pixies.
- ➤ Photo placement: There are innumerable ways of brightening wooden photo placements. Try different things with buttons, dabs, strips, paint, stickers, or sparkle. At the point when your creation is finished, add a photograph of you and the children as a token of your time together.
- ➤ Pastel hearts: A silicone shape can give new life to old colored pencil bits that would somehow get thrown out. Many children love involving the new shapes in their specialty projects.
- ➤ Espresso can drum: Old espresso jars make normal instruments. You can help your grandchildren finish the drums with paper, paint, stickers, froth, or whatever else you have available. On the off chance that you don't have covers, inflatables extended

across the highest point of the can will likewise work.

➢ Boat: It's really simple to make boats out of plastic plates, wooden sticks, and paper. Urge the children to be inventive while designing their banners. Then, at that point, have a go at dashing them in a neighborhood stream!

➢ Indoor boomerang: You can put lightweight boomerangs together with paper, so they won't harm anything. Attempt various plans to see which one flies the best.

➢ Finger manikins: These can be as much enjoyable to play with as they are to make. You can make charming plans out of paper, felt, or considerably elastic gloves

Nine

Get Artful

Any age is a decent age for creating. With modest supplies and a little creative mind, you can de-stress, have a great time, and be glad for what you make. So, feel free to begin!